About the Author

Linda Winning-Wyatt is a mother, grandmother and a sufferer. She was once a business owner of a successful cleaning business, cleaning after huge events, offices and homes, to the highest standards. She had staff under her and worked most days between ten and twelve hours. Then Fibromyalgia took its hold and everything changed.

Fibromyalgia and Me from a Charity Viewpoint

Linda Winning-Wyatt
Cardiff and Vale Fibrofighters

Fibromyalgia and Me from a
Charity Viewpoint

Olympia Publishers
London

www.olympiapublishers.com
OLYMPIA PAPERBACK EDITION

First Published in 2021

Olympia Publishers
Tallis House
2 Tallis Street
London
EC4Y 0AB
Printed in Great Britain

Dedication

We don't wish to dedicate as such, just acknowledge the charity members as a whole for their input and encouragement.

I would also like to thank the other trustees Monique Kleuver for the idea in the first place and editorial help. My husband, Alan, for giving me the time and advice as we lay sunbathing and resting in Portugal writing the original copy and also for putting this together and typing it up.

Contents

1. Introduction

Thank you for buying this book.

We are writing this book to give those who suffer from Fibromyalgia an understanding about the condition, and for those who think they might have come to terms with their friend Fibromyalgia — or, as we like to call him, "Fibby" (F-Eye-Be).

We want to deliver an easy read that comes in small chapters as many who suffer with Fibby, have trouble concentrating for long periods and suffer on occasion with Fibro Fog (chapter 17).

Please read this book with an open mind. Many people who suffer from Fibby feel useless and unworthy; it is not "all in your head" as many people will tell you, but it does start there (chapter 7).

If you feel like trying some of the ideas after reading this book, please ask your doctor before doing so. We as Trustees of Cardiff and Vale Fibrofighters, are not medical experts, so you must check with your doctor first. In our groups, we have found that what works for one doesn't work for another, and that what is safe for one could be dangerous for another.

Our Medical Disclaimer states that everyone should refer to their doctor before trying any advice given, as we are not medical professionals.

Finally, we hope you find this book informative.

The Trustees of Cardiff and Vale Fibrofighters

2. Cardiff and Vale Fibrofighters

Cardiff and Vale Fibrofighters was started by four people who suffer, getting together to have coffee and to find friends who also have Fibromyalgia in their lives.

Over the months, our group began to get bigger and bigger. People from Barry asked about starting a group there, so we advertised to see if there was any interest. Monique Kleuver, one of the Trustees, and two other members joined and over the following weeks the group continued to grow.

One week, after a group meeting, Monique, myself (Linda Winning-Wyatt) and my husband-come-carer Alan, decided that the next step would be to try to make the group into an official charity.

This turned out to be quite a lengthy process, involving meetings and conversations with our local MP, Alun Cairns, and local Councillor, Jane Hutt. We also had help from GVS (Glamorgan Voluntary Services).

The main aim of the charity is to run face-to-face support groups where we look after and help fellow Fibromyalgia sufferers, so that they feel less isolated and alone.

As so many people feel that "no one understands", we also welcome family and carers to these groups for advice, support, friendship and new information as we find it ourselves. We offer help and advocacy, as well as a sympathetic shoulder to cry on.

Our group started in 2017 and we officially registered as a charity in December 2019, so we started 2020 with a bang!

At the time of writing, we have three active groups and two more pending. We are continually approached to start new groups and never stop looking for existing groups. We have over one hundred and fifty followers on our Facebook, The Cardiff and Vale Fibromyalgia Fighters, and many more on our website at cardiffandvalefibrofighters.org.uk.

We are creating valuable resources such as PowerPoint presentations and our training has already been adopted by South Wales Police and Cardiff International Airport. We are also involved in two disability forums.

For more information:

Email us at: cardiffandvalefibrofighters@hotmail.com

Phone us on 0739 966 5245

The Trustees:
    Linda Winning-Wyatt — Chairperson
    Monique Kleuver — Treasurer/Secretary
    Alan   Winning-Wyatt—Treasurer/Campaign Manager

3. History of Fibromyalgia

Probably the first accepted description of Fibromyalgia is found in the Bible, in Job 7: 3–4 and Job 30: 16–17. "I too have been assigned months of futility, long and weary nights of misery. When I go to bed; I think when will it be morning? But the night drags on, and I toss till dawn, and now my heart is broken."

"Depression haunts my day, my weary nights are filled with pain as though something were gnawing at my bones."

Here are a few dates from history to see how and when fibromyalgia was seen as a proper condition:

1600s: Fibromyalgia-like symptoms were first given the name Muscular Rheumatism.

1816: Dr William Balfour, Surgeon at the University of Edinburgh gave the first full description of Fibromyalgia.

1824: Dr Balfour described the tender points associated with Fibromyalgia.

1854–1856: During the Crimean war, the English army nurse Florence Nightingale was taken ill with Fibromyalgia-like symptoms whilst working on the front lines. Nightingale never recovered and was virtually bedridden much of the time, suffering from unrelenting pain and fatigue until her death in 1910.

1904: Sir William Gowers coined the term Fibroitis

(which literally means inflammation of the fibres). He also denoted the tender points found in patients with Muscular Rheumatism.

1972: Dr Hugh Smyth laid the foundation of the modern definition of Fibromyalgia by describing widespread pain and tender points.

1975: The first electroencephalogram (EEG) study identifying the sleep disturbances that accompany Fibromyalgia was performed. A medical paper was first written about the condition.

1976: Because no evidence of inflammation could be found, physicians changed the name from Fibroitis to Fibromyalgia (meaning pain in the muscles and tissues).

1981: The first controlled clinical study with validation of known symptoms and tender points was published.

1987: The American Medical Association recognised Fibromyalgia as a real condition.

1990: The American College of Rheumatology developed a diagnostic criterion of Fibromyalgia to be used for research purposes. This criterion was soon being used by clinicians as a tool to help diagnose patients. Also in the 1990s, the concept of neurohormonal sensitization was developed.

2005: The first guidelines for treating Fibromyalgia pain were published by the American Pain Society.

2007: The first prescription was approved to manage Fibromyalgia.

2018: Florence Nightingale's birthday was the 12th May 1820, so Fibromyalgia Awareness Day is now on this date every year, as a reminder of her life and commitment.

4. Before Fibromyalgia

Many of our members had a good life before diagnosis and having Fibromyalgia. They were working, enjoying physical activities and socially active. Even on occasion running their own business.

As I write this, I think back to what I was doing before my diagnosis. I ran my own company with a partner, doing sometimes sixty to seventy hours a week. We cleaned properties and often cleaned up behind big events in St. Donat's Castle. Now, I can't even clean my own two-bedroom bungalow. Another Trustee owned several companies over the years but finds even the simplest things can be a hassle. A member used to have her own fruit and vegetable stall out in all weathers. She now struggles.

So, you can see that people who have Fibromyalgia are not lazy. They are not "playing the system" as so many people imagine. If anyone says this to me, I direct them to our logo: a man covered in bruises and raised veins. I suggest walking in my shoes for twenty-four hours. Then see if I am faking it.

Please read this book before making any judgement on those of us who live with Fibromyalgia.

5. So this is Fibby

Fibromyalgia, as you will see in the following chapters, is an invisible condition that affects the whole body. In one of our groups, a sufferer told us that when her niece asks how she is, she always says, "How is Fibby today? Are you beating Fibby or is he winning?" As the group listened, we all smiled and said it was a lovely way to think about the condition.

So, here is Fibby.

Let's learn a little more about him.

Fibby is a neurological disorder that affects your whole body. It normally occurs after the sufferer has experienced a stressful or traumatic experience. It can affect anyone, at anytime, anywhere, at any age.

The statistics are that:

• It affects around seven times as many women as men.

• The condition typically appears between the ages thirty and fifty.

It has been estimated that one in twenty people may have some form of Fibromyalgia.

If the condition wasn't invisible, you would see people covered in bruises and raised veins.

Over the next few chapters, we will give you a better understanding of Fibby.

Fibromyalgia

- A sense of hoplessness
- Lost of personality
- Loss of finacial Stability
- Completing Suicide
- Loss of Self Esteem
- Suicidal thought

Brain fog

Sensativities
Neurological
low mood
Timitus
Nausea
Grief
Dizzyness
vertigo
Burning
numbness
intolerance
Disturbances
CFS
Exhaustion
Visual Disturbances
unrefreshed
Allergies
restorative sleep
Not believed

WIDE SPREAD PAIN
muscle weakness
Communication Problems
Tingling
Twitches
Not Respected
muscle spasm
irritable bowel & bladder
Social excluded
Coldness
Feeling bruised
Restless leg syndrome
Stiffness
Balance issues

- Life is over
- Anxiety about Futur
- Fear
- Loss of social confidence
- Loss of Self worth
- Loss of Self respect

- Loss of social invitations
- Social Stigma
- Lack of Empathy & Understanding
- pathological

2nd me!

- Bargaining Good & Bad day

muscle cramps
mimicking five symptoms

Fibromyalyia IS Real

6. Fibby and Me

In this chapter, we are going to look at how Fibby shares lives and how sometimes it takes complete control.

The gingerbread figure on the previous page shows you that Fibby doesn't just live in part of you: Fibby gets into all of your body. When this occurs, it is known as a "Fibro Flare". We will look at words associated with Fibby in chapter 9.

A flare can hit you at any time and always comes when you least expect it. These flares can last ages or can go as quickly as they came. There doesn't seem to be any pattern to them.

Later, we will explain some ways to manage flares, what we have found makes it worse and what seems to make it better.

The best explanations of a flare are:

"I feel like I have been in the ring with Mike Tyson" or

"I feel like I have been hit by a truck".

We hope that you can see a flare is not just the normal aches and pains a sufferer has to cope with.

7. Symptoms of Fibromyalgia

- Musculoskeletal Pain
- Tender Points
- Stiffness
- Fatigue
- Non-Restorative Sleep
- Difficulty Focusing
- Ankylosing Spondylitis
- Anxiety
- Bladder Problems
- Coping with Fatigue Syndrome
- Dizziness/Balance Problems
- Dry Mouth
- Extra Sensitivity to Noise/Light/Food
- Gynaecological Problems—Endometriosis/Painful Periods/Volvodynia
- Underactive Thyroid
- Lower Back Pain
- I.B.S. (Irritable Bowel Syndrome)
- Multiple Chemical Sensitivity
- Muscle Twitches and Cramp Spasms
- Myofasical Pain Syndrome
- Numbness/Tingling of Hands and Feet
- Post Traumatic Syndrome Disease
- Restless Leg Syndrome

- Rheumatoid Arthritis
- Sleep Apnoea
- Systemic Lupus Erythemastous
- Painful/Frequent Passing of Urine
- Temporomandibular Joint Disorder
- Tinnitus
- Tension Migraine Headaches
- Temperature Sensitivity

As you can see from this non-exhaustive list, it is not plain sailing.

The 18 Trigger points of diagnosing Fibromyalgia

1. Lower right on neck front ① ②
2. Edge right upper chest ③
3. Lower left neck in the front
4. On the edge of upper chest. ⑤
5. Bone on the right side below ar elbow ④
6. Bone of the left hand side below the elbow ⑥
7. Just above the knee on inside of leg ⑦ ⑧
8. Just above the right knee on the inside of leg

Front

9. The left base of skull
10. The right base of skull
11. Neck + the shoulders
12. left + right
13) Both upper inner
14) Shoulders
15) The outer part of your buttock both sides
16) of your buttock both sides
17) Both sides of your hip
18) of your hip bone.

Back

This a guideline to give Rheumatology. They use this guide when making a diagnosis of FIBROMYALGIA if the patient has a score of over 11 when touched on these various pressure points

23

8. How and when do I get Diagnosed?

A diagnosis often takes a long time due to the fact that the doctor usually will do a lot of tests, blood tests, scans and similar to rule out other possible illnesses.

The doctor will end up diagnosing you with Fibromyalgia when they cannot find anything else. Therefore, we as a group recommend that you get a second opinion from a rheumatologist, to confirm the diagnosis. Get a written copy, as you may need it in the future.

A rheumatologist will normally check out the "Tender Points" that are given as an outline by medical associations (see over for a diagram of these points). They will check how many of these points you have pain in and, if you react to more than twelve out of eighteen and have the other symptoms mentioned in the last chapter, they will diagnose Fibromyalgia.

Some rheumatologists will provide you with a leaflet and send you on your way. This is what happened to me: I was sent away with a rough diagnosis and a piece of paper. It felt good to have the diagnosis and assurance that I was not a hypochondriac!

I know many fellow sufferers have had similar experiences, which is one reason we started the charity. Some have said:

"At long last, a name. I am not going mad!"

"Why me?"

"Where can I get help?"

"Phew! It is not all in my head!"

I know when I was diagnosed, I felt a weight lifted off my shoulders. At thirteen, I was diagnosed with an underactive thyroid after my mum had said to the hospital staff, "I don't want her back home until you find out what is wrong with her."

I was kept in hospital for two weeks before they diagnosed me with a mix of underactive thyroid and glandular fever. I lived with an underactive thyroid for over thirty years. My test levels would never come out right, so I was referred to see a specialist at Barts Hospital in London when I was pregnant with each of my three children, to make sure that everything stayed OK with my thyroid. Even they struggled with my levels.

I had often said that I was sure it was something else as I was having other symptoms. Eventually, after moving to Wales, a doctor diagnosed me with Fibromyalgia. I felt so alone with this illness. Even though my husband understood most of the time, other members of the family would say, "It's all in your head," or, "She is not as bad as she makes out."

One of my own children could not believe it until she worked with someone who had Fibromyalgia and saw it for herself in another person. They apologised and now are very understanding.

Some health boards offer these services to help you after your diagnosis:

• Pain Clinic

- Wellbeing Nurses
- Physiotherapy
- Dieticians

Something that helped me after my diagnosis was meeting others with Fibromyalgia. It helped me realise I was not alone.

And that's why I started the charity.

9. Handy Words Associated with Fibromyalgia

Flare-up: A flare-up describes when all the symptoms are actively at their worst.

Brain Fog: Brain Fog describes your memory, thoughts, and words — how you can get half way through a conversation or doing something and forget the simplest of things.

Tender Points: Tender Points is the term used by doctors for the areas of your body that hurt when pushed. Rheumatologists look for these during their examination, for diagnosis.

IBS: Irritable Bowel Syndrome, a common problem associated with Fibromyalgia. It affects your digestive system.

Non-Restorative Sleep: Another common symptom. Fibromyalgia sufferers often cannot fall into deep sleep, so their body does not heal itself or restore lost energy.

EEG: Electroencephalogram, a test to see the electrical activity of the brain and to record its levels.

EMG: Electromyography, a technique for evaluating and recording electrical activity produced by the muscles.

MRI: Magnetic Response Imaging, a scan using very strong magnetic fields and radio waves to produce very detailed images of the inside of a body.

Vitamins B and D: Often taken as part of treatment, as deficiencies are a symptom of Fibromyalgia.

10. Helpful Questions for the Rheumatologist

- How do I know I have Fibromyalgia?
- What medicines can I take? Are there any side effects?
- What food, drugs and activities should I avoid?
- What exercise is helpful?
- What alternative therapies are there that might help?
- How do I explain my condition to my family and friends?
- Are there any stress-management techniques that help?
- Would you recommend counselling?
- Can you recommend a support group and/or online community?
- Are there any trials running at the moment?

Even though these questions are for the rheumatologist, we will try to answer some of them through this book.

We also know that you can go with all good intentions then clam up on the day, so don't panic.

11. What Next?

So, I have Fibby in my body… what next?

A lot of our members have said that they started by joining online forums but soon found these tended to be depressing, as they were just consisted of paragraphs after paragraphs of symptoms. For example, the constant "Do you have pain here? I have pain there," discussions.

This is good to an extent, but can soon be depressing and monotonous. Members have all said that it is lovely to meet up face-to-face with fellow sufferers, to feel less alone with their daily battle against Fibby. We had one young lady in her twenties sit in the group for around half an hour, then burst into tears. Not what a leader of the group wants or expects! However, when we asked if everything was OK, she said:

"I have sat here and listened to everyone. I am so relieved I am not the only one with these symptoms. I am not going mad!"

So, my advice would be to find a support group doing face-to-face meetings in your area and try it out. If you can't find one, please contact us and we will try to find one for you or even start a new group under our "umbrella name" if someone can keep it running.

Another way to help yourself is by reading books or going on Google and doing research. This can be good and bad: there is so much information out there and so many conditions overlap. This can be confusing and you may recognise symptoms in yourself that are not actually part of the condition. What I am saying is look and learn, but be careful. Too much information can sometimes be a bad thing!

12. Learning to live with Fibby

We always say that learning to live with Fibby is a bit like bereavement. You have lost your old life and now you have to learn how to live all over again. So, give yourself time to learn new ways.

In a future chapter, we will go into coping mechanisms.

13. How to Deal with Fibby

This chapter looks at ways to deal with Fibby, and ways of avoiding flare-ups. Nothing is guaranteed as your body is unique to you, so what works for you may not work for someone else, and vice versa.

De-stress

We know that the society we live in — especially in 2020 when writing this — is stressful for most people. Yet this is one of the biggest triggers for setting Fibby off. So, if you can, minimise your stress. Some ways to get your stress levels down are yoga, careful exercise, getting sleep regularly and meditation/breathing exercises. We will look further into this in chapter 19. You must already know some things that work for you, such as taking a bath or going out for a walk with the dog.

Write it down

If your Fibro Fog (chapter 17) is making you unable to remember or focus on a task, write yourself a list. Keep this near you and tick off as you do things. Keep a pad and pen by the bed to jot down your thoughts during those sleepless periods. Make lists of jobs to do through the day, things to remember to tell your partner when they return, shopping lists and so on and so on. It may sound silly but do it, even if it is only two items. I have many times gone into a supermarket just to think "Why am I here?"

Exercise regularly

Exercise is the one thing that we all dread as sufferers and is often the worst thing to do when going through a flare-up. However, doing gentle exercise can often ease the symptoms, making you feel better. Something simple like taking a gentle stroll around the block or aqua aerobics, which is particularly good as the water takes your weight. Exercise often helps with sleep, too. Talk this through with your doctor to create an exercise plan.

Serious soaking

Soaking yourself in a hot bath or hot tub can relax you, helping to ease the joints and muscles and regain movement. If you don't have a bath, try using a stool in your shower; sit under a pressure setting and let the water do its work. Moist heat encourages endorphins, which block pain and help you sleep.

De-caffeinate yourself

Caffeine is a compound that increases stress, both physically and psychologically. It stimulates the heart and your central nervous system, potentially increasing nervousness, anxiety and insomnia. De-caffeinate and de-stress. Little known fact: there is more caffeine in tea than coffee. Watch out for caffeine in chocolate, fizzy drinks and other products. Reduce the amount or cut it out altogether, if you can.

Take some me-time

Fibby often poses unique challenges and makes your life complicated. So, make sure you give yourself "me-time". Lose yourself in a hobby, listen to music, watch television. This allows your body time to gather both energy and de-stress. Getting a good balance in life's routine is essential.

Fibby and work

Try to tell your boss, as it can open up options for flexi-plans or flexi-time, helping you become more productive at work and not a hindrance in the boss's eyes. Rearranging your desk furniture for comfort and easy accessibility can often help, too. Work doesn't always understand and you may need a visit to HR or your Union to get help.

Talk about it

Fibby is stressful enough for you and those around you. Communication is essential; don't put on a happy face to avoid difficulties. People need to know what makes things worse. Try to have conversations when you are at your best. Try to focus on one issue at a time as confusion is part and parcel of Fibby. Search for answers and don't be afraid to ask for help, as others have often been in similar situations.

Make your bedroom a sleep sanctuary

If you are having trouble sleeping, you may need to reserve the room purely for sleeping. Remove the television and computer. Make the area as peaceful as you can. Make sure it is dark, quiet and cool. Keep distractions as low as possible so, once you have soaked in your bath, you can relax in your sanctuary.

Other things that might help;

Learn to say no

Keep a diary

Join a support group.

14. Fibro Flares

A typical Fibro Flare is how we (and the medical profession) talk about a bad day.

When Fibby pains flare up, every activity can seem more difficult. Flares can affect the Fibro Fog, too. All of us experience flares differently and there can be different triggers depending on each person.

Some people have regular flares; if this happens, they are not all the same and fluctuate in intensity.

Flares can happen at any time, without warning, although they tend to happen during times of stress or pressure.

Flare-ups often last anywhere from a few days to a week, but can come as quickly as they go.

Here are a few triggers we have found can start a flare-up:

Diet, hormones, physical or psychological stress, change of schedule, temperature changes, weather changes and new treatments.

Other things are stressful events such as a surgery or an accident. These tend to make symptoms worse. Lack of sleep and even not exercising enough can also cause symptoms to worsen.

15. Can I Get Better from Fibby?

As a group, we would love to say, "Yes!", but I am afraid at present we would be lying to you. Also, if we were perfectly honest with you, we don't see a miracle cure happening in the near future, due to how much of a complex a condition Fibby is. We do, however, hope after reading this book you will have a better understanding of "How to live with Fibby".

Through the last four years, I have learnt ways to manage Fibby through doing various therapies. One of these is:

The Spoon Therapy

You may be laughing at the name but most people who have tried this find it very useful.

Imagine you hold ten spoons (or if you prefer, do it literally). It makes no difference what type of spoon. These spoons are in your hands at the beginning of your day. You have them before you get out of bed or do anything. You have ten spoons a day. Are you with me so far?

Some days you can get out of bed with ease. This might only take one spoon away. However, another day you ache all over and feel as if your body has been hit by a truck. This may take three to four spoons. Understand so far?

Next you have to wash and dress — on a not-so-good day this may take two to three spoons.

So, looking at this scenario on a not-good day, you've already used five to seven spoons out of ten!

It is all about learning to pace yourself and accept that taking breaks when your spoons get to around two to three, is both sensible and necessary. Take a break, make a coffee (decaffeinated), sit for half an hour. You may gain you a spoon or two.

Another idea that works is to plan ahead. If you are aware that a busy day is coming up, rest the day before to build up your spoons.

Spoon Therapy only works if you take it seriously and listen to your body. Only you know your own body.

Other things that may boost your spoon count are:

Relaxation	Yoga
Massage	Swimming
Meditation	Music
Tai Chi	Reflexology
Quietness	Reiki

Some of these things might help you but not someone else; everyone is different. Remember our medical disclaimer that tells you to **always speak to your doctor before trying anything new**. We are not medical professionals.

Everything is trial and error; see what works and what doesn't. Don't risk trying anything without professional backing. Look after yourself. You are the only person who you can truly rely on. If something gives you five minutes of help, then that is better than nothing.

16. Medication

Fibromyalgia and medication are a very personal relationship. A consultant at a local hospital who specialises in Fibromyalgia and pain once said:

"If you are prescribed a medicine that isn't helping you, see your doctor, stop taking them and try something else. Your health is important. You only have one life, make the best of it. One medicine works for one person and not another. Listen to your body."

Medication often given to Fibby patients includes:

Painkillers

Simple over-the-counter painkillers may help to relieve the pain associated with Fibby. However, not all may be suitable to every sufferer so always ask the pharmacist and read the leaflet inside the package before taking them.

When over-the-counter tablets don't help, your doctor or consultant may prescribe you stronger tablets, such as codeine (e.g., Tramadol). However, these tablets can be addictive and their effects weaken over time. This means that to keep the level of pain relief increase is necessary.

Don't take any tablet not prescribed by your doctor.

Never stop taking prescribed tablets outright. You need to wean yourself off a lot of them. Also never stop and start, leaving gaps in between: this can cause serious problems.

Antidepressants

Antidepressants can also help with pain caused by Fibby. This is done by increasing chemicals that send messages to the brain known as neurotransmitters. It is believed that having low neurotransmitters is one symptom of Fibby, so increasing these chemicals increases the levels, thus, reducing pain throughout the body for a Fibby sufferer.

The medication your doctor or consultant uses will depend on the severity of your symptoms.

Tricyclic antidepressants such as Amitriptyline.

Serotonin-Norodrenaline Reuptake Inhibitors (SNRIs), such as Duloxetine and Venlafaxine.

Selective Serotonin Reuptake Inhibitors (SSRIs), such as Fluoxetine (Prozac) and Paroxetine.

A medication called Pramipexole, which is not a depressant but also affects the levels of neurotransmitters, can be used as well.

Antidepressants do have side effects that we will look at in the next chapter.

Medication to help you sleep

Fibby sufferers often have trouble sleeping, so you may want to try a medicine that helps you sleep. Some antidepressants can boost your sleep. Talk this through with your doctor before trying over-the-counter medicines.

Muscle relaxants

If you suffer from spasms or stiffness in your muscles due to Fibby, your doctor or consultant may prescribe a short course of muscle relaxants such as diazepam. This medicine often improves sleep due to its sedative effect.

Anticonvulsants

Another medicine you may be given is an anticonvulsant (anti-seizure) as these can help the symptoms of Fibby. The most common medicines used for Fibby are Pregablin and Gapapentin.

These medicines are normally for cases of epilepsy but research has shown that some Fibby patients have had improved symptoms from their use. These drugs also have side effects (next chapter).

Antipsychotics

Antipsychotic medicines, also called neuroleptics, are sometimes used to help relieve long-term pain in Fibby patients. This still needs more research to confirm, yet new medicines are being found to help this complex condition.

Research is taking place all over the world, including in England.

17. Side Effects

Many medicines carry side effects that you have to deal with on top of your illness.

Listed below are the most commonly used medicines for the care of Fibby and their side effects.

Name	Common Side Effects	Rare Side Effects
Paroxetine	Drowsiness Dry mouth Sexual dysfunction	Increased risk of suicide 25 or below Serotonin syndrome
Amitriptyline	Blurred vision Constipation Dry mouth Gait disturbances Sedation	Increased risk of suicide 25 or below Heart arrhythmias Lower blood count
Duloxetine	Constipation Diarrhoea Dizziness Dry mouth Headaches Stomach upset Sweating	Increased risk of suicide 25 or below Serotonin syndrome Rapid Heart Rate

Gabapentin	Blurred vision
	Confusion
	Dizziness
	Liver/Kidney problems
	Lack of concentration
	Swelling

Pregablin   Heart Failure

(Information from Medshadow.org)

Please be aware of these symptoms and if you have any, advise your doctor or consultant.

18. Let's Talk About Fibro Fog

Fibro Fog is one of the more annoying issues with sufferers. In this chapter, we will look at why it happens, when it happens and what exactly the term Fibro Fog means.

So, what is Fibro Fog?

As you have read this book and seen that the condition has many stems to it, you will have noticed that sufferers have lots to cope with — widespread pain, fatigue, sleep and mood issues being just a few. Lack of sleep affects the body in several ways, one of which is "Fibro Fog".

Fibro Fog is a collection of cognitive difficulties common in sufferers of Fibby. It can lead to problems with memory, being able to think clearly and simply forgetting the simplest of things.

Research has shown that more than half of Fibromyalgia sufferers will have a decline in their memory and clarity of thinking. Sufferers often say that they simply can't find the words they want to use, often getting sentences back to front or mixed up without realising it.

Here's a short list of a few other things you might experience:

• Memory issues — forgetfulness

- Impaired ability to concentrate or stay focused
- Decreased alertness
- Problems thinking clearly or mental slowness
- Difficulty holding conversations

Research also shows a deficit in what are known as *Executive Functioning Skills*, such as planning abilities, decision-making and abstract thinking. Sufferers say that the significant impact that Fibro Fog has can be more disabling than the pain itself. Many have even gone as far as thinking that they had dementia.

So, what causes Fibro Fog?

Scientists doing research into the brain are at present still unsure why Fibro Fog occurs. However, here are three possibilities:

- Chronic pain demands attention, which in turn demands a marked mental effort. This could contribute to reducing the cognitive processing resources available and therefore have an effect on performance on the cognitive task at hand.

- Fibromyalgia is a neurological condition. Therefore, an irregularity in the way certain neurological paths and neurotransmitters function within the brain may also play a role in cognitive issues.

- Fibro Fog may also be associated with other aspects of Fibromyalgia.

Poor sleep

Sleep patterns in a sufferer are often disturbed by pain and some also have other disorders, such as *restless leg syndrome* and *sleep apnoea*. If you are not sleeping correctly, it is safe to assume that this will affect your mental processing functions.

Depression

Unfortunately, this is a common issue with sufferers and could be another factor, although research would need to confirm this.

19. Help that may relieve Fibro Fog

Exercise

Exercise has been found to be one of the best treatments; it has been shown that physical exercise over a long period improves cognitive processing as well as other symptoms.

Start exercise slowly then gradually build up. There are various options, such as water aerobics, swimming or just walking. Your doctor or consultant can advise you of what would be of most benefit to you. They can also have a plan made up for you.

Brain workouts

You can do this with puzzles of various types, playing games and other mentally stimulating activities. It has been said that it is just as important to exercise your brain as it is your body.

Sleep schedule

It is important to create and keep a regular sleep schedule as this helps by regulating your body clock. Having enough sleep can also help with the repair of your body functions, both mentally and physically. Other things that might help your sleep pattern may be avoiding naps, limiting your caffeine intake and avoiding playing electronic games or watching television just before bed.

Habits that might help your Fibro Fog

- Try not to do too much at once
- Avoid distractions when doing a task
- Pace yourself; use Spoon Therapy
- Make time for relaxation every day

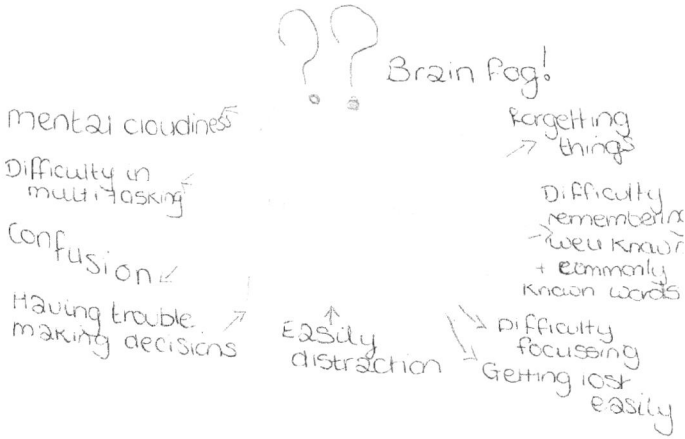

?? Brain Fog!

mental cloudiness

Difficulty in multitasking

Confusion

Having trouble making decisions

Forgetting things

Difficulty remembering well known + commonly known words

Easily distraction

Difficulty focussing

Getting lost easily

20. Food

In this chapter, we will be looking at foods that help the symptoms of Fibby, and those foods that make the symptoms worse. This information is just that and you should see your Dietician or Wellbeing Nurse as they have a better knowledge around this subject. Also, giving up things may be bad for you as you may need them for medical reasons or for health reasons.

Foods Fibby Likes

Vegetables and fruit — Try to eat the average eight to nine a day.

Whole grains — Barley, buckwheat, oats, quinoa, brown rice, wheat and spelt.

These foods provide vitamins, protein and fibre.

Healthy oil — Olive oil is a good choice.

Herbs and spices — Many herbs and spices contain antioxidants, which can reduce inflammation. Turmeric, bay leaves, cinnamon and many others may offer benefits.

Turmeric may also help people with rheumatoid arthritis.

Vitamin D

New research has found a link between Fibromyalgia symptoms and a deficiency in vitamin D.

Some good sources of vitamin D:

Egg yolks, low fat yoghurt fortified with vitamin D, orange juice, swordfish, salmon, tuna, whole grain cereal fortified with vitamin D.

Foods with vitamin D may not reduce symptoms in everyone with Fibby, but at least you will have stronger bones!

The Mediterranean diet is rich in fruits, fish, vegetables and anti-inflammatory food.

Foods Fibby Doesn't Like

A number of additives and ingredients may make your symptoms worse.

Meat and dairy

People who suffer from Fibby may find it helps to limit their daily intake because many dairy products contain saturated fat. You could try opting for low-fat versions or dairy alternatives such as soya milk.

You may find it helps to limit the amount of red meat you eat. Try eating turkey, fish and vegetables instead, although red meat is good for you as a source of nutrients such as B12 and iron — your body needs these nutrients as they help produce new red blood cells.

Red meat is also high in protein, which is needed for building strong muscles, bones and other tissues. It also builds enzymes. The bad side of eating red meat is that eating too much regularly can cause health problems like *heart disease, some cancers, kidney function problems and digestive issues.*

Additives

According to research, food additives called excitotoxin may worsen Fibby symptoms.

Examples of these are:

MSG: monosodium glutamate, a flavour enhancer.

Aspartame: an artificial sweetener (e.g., Canderel).

Gluten: some research suggests that gluten may also affect various inflammatory conditions.

Other ingredients that may trigger inflammation include saturated fats and trans fats, refined starches and foods with added sugar.

Our suggestion once again is to speak to your health specialist (Wellbeing Nurse or Doctor) before trying any new diet of any kind. Keep a diary of what you are eating, the time you ate it and the reaction it caused in your body. Each person reacts differently; you are unique.

21. Exercise

Exercise is a swear word for many people, especially sufferers of Fibromyalgia and especially during a flare-up or when simply exhausted.

However, you may find it helps and makes you feel better!

It all depends on how severe the pain is at the time. It can work by helping you concentrate on something other than the pain. As an example, taking a stroll with a friend or family member often involves chatting and laughter — you're getting exercise but you aren't thinking about it as exercise.

Other activities

Tai Chi

Aerobics (to your ability, which may mean seated exercise)

Yoga

Swimming (one of the best exercises as the water takes your weight)

We as a charity are thinking of making a short DVD or PowerPoint presentation with the help of a personal trainer, covering various exercises that may improve your pain management.

22. Therapists Who May Offer You Help

We are very aware that it can be hard to get the services you need and which may help in the UK. Yet there are experienced professionals out there to help you have and live a better life.

Physiotherapist

They specialise in the movement of muscles and joints. Provide exercise plans and information.

Occupational Therapist

The skill sector here is around safety. These people help to find ways to help around the house. To do with balance and safety, such as grab rails.

Counsellor

Their skills are in the mind. These individuals will help you to cope after a traumatic experience. This is done through various ways of looking at the situation and then working new patterns around the situation.

Chiropractor

These professionals are trained around the musculoskeletal system. They can help to manipulate muscles and joints after an injury and build the area up again.

Cognitive Behavioural Therapist

CBT is a therapy in which you re-train your thoughts to manage problems. This helps by changing the way you think and behave.

Wellbeing Nurse

These professionals work alongside doctors, offering help in maintaining your wellbeing. They offer various services like mindfulness, chair yoga and food and nutrition classes.

To find the full range of classes available, contact the doctor responsible for your Wellbeing Nurses directly. Your doctor will have the address of your nearest surgery offering courses and what's on at the moment.

Like with many services in today's society, not all Fibby friends will have access to all these helpful services. It is always good to see your doctor and chat about what help and services are available in your area.

23. Other Services

Physiotherapist

Provide crutches and walking sticks.

Support Worker

You may be able to get help from a support worker through social services. We as a charity provide support workers who will help with various documents such as claims for Personal Independence Payment (PIP). They also will attend medical appointments and reviews, help with advocacy and do odd jobs to help out.

Citizens Advice Bureau

The help that this organisation provides is with debt, housing and legal problems. Their phone number is at the back of the book, along with other useful contacts.

Chemist/Pharmacist

These individuals concern themselves with medication. They can arrange with your doctor to collect your prescription and deliver your medicines straight to your house. They can also pre-pack your medicines in the prescribed doses in individual blister packs if you have difficulty remembering what tablets to take and when. You can also buy boxes from them that hold your tablets in individual dose sections.

Care 'N' Repair

This is a group normally run by your local council.

They are people who will come and do repairs to your property and things like that.

We always recommend finding a professional if there is anything needing doing in your house that you are not qualified to undertake.

24. Things it May be Better to Avoid

Weather

The weather can have an adverse effect on your pain levels, especially rain, mist, wind, cold and damp.

If you can avoid going out on days like these, it will help your joints and muscles.

Stress

This is a big problem for Fibby sufferers. Stress will make your whole body worse. Stress is the main cause of flare-ups.

Excitement

You may find that you suffer the next day due to the adrenaline rush, during the time of excitement.

Over-exertion

Pushing your body too hard can also cause flare-ups.

Look back at chapter 14: Spoon Therapy. It is so important as a sufferer of Fibby to pace yourself.

Never easy and very frustrating, but necessary.

25. How to Tell Family and Work About Fibby

To be honest, members of the group agree that this is actually worse than being diagnosed because you are never sure what reaction you will get.

In many cases you will get mostly negative comments to start with, like:

"It's all in your head."

"There is no such thing."

"You don't look bad."

"Hypochondriac!"

"You are just lazy…"

"I guess you don't really want to work."

"It can't be that bad."

This is hard to take as you are still coming to terms with the reality of the condition. Ask any sufferer. They will honestly say that all those statements are based on myths.

Of course, there are people who will put it on and "work the system" — and these people are the reason genuine sufferers have such a hard time.

As the condition becomes better recognised, so has the number of naysayers decreased. Several famous people are now recognising that they have Fibromyalgia: Lady Gaga is probably the most famous role model for

Fibromyalgia in America.

You will see as we move on in chapter 24 (How to deal with disbelievers) that with more information comes better defence. And in chapter 25, we'll cover 10 ways to understand how Fibromyalgia feels.

The negative opinions are one of the reasons we decided to write this book: to help others understand what it is all about. We don't want sympathy. We want people to understand better and be less judgemental. That would go a long way!

The most important thing you can do is **be honest with everyone**. The worst thing you can do (and most of us have done this) is put a smile on your face and say, "I'm fine." That really doesn't help anyone as no one knows how to respond. They already suspect that you are not fine, but you say that you are.

Try to open up as much as you can to your partner, family and friends as the more real you are with them, the more real they can be with you. My mum used to say to my husband:

"Take everything with a pinch of salt. She is not that bad."

However, recently my mother and I went away on a break together and she finally began to recognise the limits my condition puts on me. She witnessed just how little I was able to do and the pain I was in. That break changed her mindset and her attitude towards me.

Please do try to be honest with everyone. In the long run, you will help all concerned.

26. How to Deal with Disbelievers

Although Fibromyalgia awareness is increasing, along with research into its existence, it is still very hard for many people to believe in. Fibromyalgia is invisible and everyone with Fibby looks healthy.

First off, it is a problem as... what do you call it? Is it a condition, an illness, a disease or just a diagnosis?

Also, as previously said, most people will react with various levels of mockery and disbelief. Whether it is a new doctor, an old friend, a member of the family or a work colleague, it is just as hard to swallow your hurt at their disbelief.

Try to remember that their reaction is due to ignorance and is not an attack on you personally.

From the easiest to the hardest, we will try to give you ways to deal with everyone who needs to understand: doctors, friends, bosses, colleagues and even family and your spouse.

Doctors

A number of reputable doctors and researchers find it hard to believe in Fibby as a disease. Although they struggle with what is actually wrong with you, they do not deny your symptoms. The problem they have is the many theories of what causes Fibby; none have been proved conclusively. Therefore, many doctors are reluctant to accept Fibby; they like facts, not theories, and are hesitant to name the condition.

When you come across such a doctor, remember they believe in your symptoms. They are not calling you a liar or a lazy person. They are simply playing it safe. On the other hand, there are doctors who genuinely do not believe that anything to do with Fibby is real. Odds are they don't think you're faking your symptoms but if you come across one that does (they are out there) turn around and walk out of their office, never to return.

Friends

The next easiest are your friends. Compared to the rest of the list, doctors are easy as you can just turn around and walk away. You don't have an emotional investment to worry about.

Friends who knew you before you had the condition normally fall into two categories:

1. They have prior misconceptions about the condition or,

2. They have googled and found loads of the rubbish out there calling it a lie anyway.

You best reaction, even if it is hard in the situation, is to stay calm. Let your friend know how painful their disbelief is to you; show them a medical leaflet on Fibromyalgia. You can pick these up at pain clinics and neurology departments. Tell them that you understand their feelings as the condition has only recently been recognised but also that, right now, you really need their understanding and support.

Once they have read the leaflet, ask them if they have any questions. Try to answer them honestly. Avoid anything that sounds like whining.

If after all this, they still won't believe you then you really need to cut them loose. Developing Fibromyalgia comes with it a lot of pain and hardships.

Boss

Working with the condition can be very challenging and there are many who physically can't even consider carrying on in their work — or any regular work. If you are one of the lucky ones who can physically cope or you work in a job that has flexibility and makes allowances for your condition, then great!

Even in that environment, you need to consider "coming out" and telling your boss. We advise that telling them of your new condition can be vitally important. The only other choice — and in our opinion not a good one — is to tell your work colleagues and not the boss. They will be the ones covering for you during sickness and need to be behind you.

Like your friends, your boss may have preconceived ideas about Fibby. The best thing you can do is give them the medical information leaflet. Some won't want to read it, so, see if your doctor can arrange to speak with your boss, or write them a note. If a doctor says that the condition is serious, it is hard for someone outside of the medical profession to deny the effects.

Lastly, if your boss is staunchly resistant and refuses to make necessary allowances, it may be time to consider a new job. To try to continue working as you did before the condition will only make you worse.

Colleagues

Unlike your boss, your colleagues don't necessarily

need to know about the condition. You have to consider how frank you want to be with them, based on your comfort levels and how much will Fibby affect your interpersonal relationships at work.

To "come out" doesn't guarantee that they will believe in your condition. In this case, you can openly admit that the condition was misdiagnosed in the past but now diagnoses have improved. In the last twenty years, great leaps in research have made, with around eighty percent of doctors aware of Fibromyalgia. It may not be advisable to share leaflets or your doctor's number with co-workers, but to say that CT scans can see a difference in the brain of a sufferer might be enough to keep them quiet.

Finally, if after all this your co-workers are still abusive and unwilling to accept your condition, you need to make a choice: continue working there or leave and find another job.

Family

It can be very difficult indeed to handle your diagnosis with such a life-changing condition with a group of people you cannot simply walk away from.

Your family will probably google everything they can find on Fibby.

However, they need to be unbiased to find the real facts as it is too easy to get the wrong answers. Simply searching for "*Is Fibromyalgia real?*", will produce a number of articles telling you why it is not. They will also find many stories of things that "caused it", including but not limited to finding bacteria in the stomach, dehydration, excess weight, poor eating habits, lack of exercise, drinking, smoking, vitamin deficiencies…

We can tell you that, assuming you were diagnosed correctly, fixing those things may help but won't make the condition magically disappear.

Your first move should be to direct family to the medical leaflet and research online. Invite them to come with you to your doctor's appointments. They can get their answers direct from a medical professional and not you.

Lastly, you need to open up and be straight with them about how you feel and your need for them to be there for you and support you through this. If all this fails, then you need to limit your contact with them and explain why. You can't control them. You can only control yourself.

Spouse

I can't imagine what it would be like to suffer with this condition and have my partner disbelieve me. Most partners will go through a short period of difficulty believing as you have suddenly changed.

I also can't imagine how difficult it must be for the partner who has to watch the differences it makes. To see that medication doesn't seem to help. To find those articles that say the condition is not real.

Your first thing to address is whether your partner believes in your symptoms.

If it is only the diagnosis they struggle with, then give them the medical material to read. Ask them, implore if you have to, to come with you to your doctor's appointments. There they can ask all they want.

Join online support groups or a support group in your area. Cardiff and Vale Fibrofighters are always looking to open new groups but these need to be run by someone in the area. They are excellent opportunities to meet others who have gone through similar experiences.

On the other hand, if your partner has difficulty accepting your symptoms, this is much more difficult. You will have to ask them why they think you are lying and what benefit lying gives you. Explain that it is invisible but real. Developing the condition was one of the hardest things I went through and likely it is for you, too. You need to tell your partner this and that you really need their support with the whole thing. The sad fact is that not all relationships can survive Fibby.

Conclusion

Most importantly, it is vital that you realise that Fibby is here to stay, whatever happens. The majority of sufferers will have it for life. It is not worth the upset and difficulty of trying to convince those that can't or won't be convinced. It is a life-altering condition so take care of you first, then others.

27. Ways to Understand How Fibby Feels

1. Make a daily list of ten things you must achieve. However, only accomplish four things on each list.

2. Stay awake for forty-eight hours. Now find yourself the dullest book you can. You must read this book from start to finish.

3. Walk in socks on a plush carpet, dragging your feet as harshly as you can. Touch a metal doorknob and think about the pain that shock caused. Now repeat the exercise. And again. And again…

4. Check your bank account and find £10,000 missing overnight. Make an appointment with the manager. Get passed to customer services, who pass you to someone else, then someone else, then someone else, then someone else…

This one I think I need to explain. Fibromyalgia is still somewhat of a mystery. I really can't count the number of places I went to be told, "I don't know what is wrong with you," only to be sent off to another place to hear the same thing. And so on and so on.

5. Run ten kilometres. You cannot train for this. Go! Go out and do it right now! No walking!

6. Turn your thermostat down ten degrees. Put extra clothes on; now turn your thermostat up ten degrees, above normal. Repeat.

7. Cancel an important date with only one hour's warning on a Friday night. Tell them you're not up to coming out. See the reaction. Do it again the following week.

8. Spend a weekend without interacting. Spend the entire two days in bed.

9. Get seriously ill six times a year, taking three sick days off work each time. Do you still have a job?

10. Cook yourself a meal three times a day. Don't eat any of them because you feel sick.

28. Getting Help from Doctors and Helping Them Understand

Getting help from doctors can sometimes be hard, often due to their lack of understanding, training or open disbelief in the condition.

When you go to the doctor and find that they follow these patterns, ask the surgery if there is another doctor available. You need someone who believes and sympathises, or your struggles have just increased.

When we started our groups in Cardiff, we took our poster around to all the doctors in the area where the meeting was taking place. To our amazement, up to eight percent said that the condition didn't exist and refused to take the poster.

We did some research and found that most doctors' surgeries had a Wellbeing Nurse, all of whom were happy to put the posters up in their surgery. This allowed referrals to happen.

Thankfully, opinions are changing due to research and our persistence in the majority of surgeries, so it is well worth speaking to your doctor and telling them about your condition. This will build their awareness of both the condition and its symptoms.

We have also spoken to one of the pain consultants in the Heath Hospital. She gave us amazing advice:

"Only you know if your meds are working, don't be afraid to ask to change them."

Fibby will affect everyone differently. Something that works for you won't help someone else. You know your own body. Speak up and ask if something can be changed. You have one life and it is hard enough already.

29. Why me?

We believe everyone who lives with Fibby asks this question — sufferer and carer alike. Here are some of the phases you are likely to experience.

Frustration

The frustration that your old life has gone.

Self-reflection

Sufferers will have many thoughts after their diagnosis:

Did working too hard cause this?

Is it genetic?

Did my wild past cause this?

Did smoking cause it?

Was it another medication that caused it?

Was it my diet?

Blame

We live in a culture of blame. It is natural to want to blame others for you getting the condition.

Stress

This is possibly the main factor behind Fibby. Stress is a silent killer. I remember one doctor describing stress like this:

"Stress is like a bottle of pop; the more you put in the bigger the pop when you finally open the lid. Open the lid and it all goes bang."

30. Available Financial Help

You may be entitled to two main government benefits: Personal Independence Payment (PIP, which replaced DLA) and Employment Support Allowance (ESA).

PIP

This is a UK government benefit for those aged between sixteen and sixty-four. It is to help sufferers with the cost of their disability. PIP is not awarded by your condition but on the effects that condition has on you on a daily basis.

You must meet certain criteria to get PIP. You can claim PIP whether you are working or not. The benefit is not means-tested and is not taxable.

ESA

You may be entitled to claim ESA. It may be worth contacting the Citizens Advise Bureau as benefits are changing to Universal Credit (see useful contacts).

One thing we would say if you are looking into claiming benefits is to make sure you get a proper diagnosis by getting a second opinion from a rheumatologist. To get PIP you will need more than just a doctor's diagnosis on its own. The more backup you can get from consultants, hospitals, physiotherapists and other professionals, the easier it will be to gain your benefits.

For those who are looking into going for PIP, here are

a few things we suggest you do:

- Make sure you have all your medical notes to hand.
- Take your repeat prescription, as your doctor will need a printout that is up to date. Also take any paperwork of past medication, as this will build your case. It also shows the length of time you have been under your doctor's care.
- Make a list of any professionals you have been seen by, the dates and what they saw you for, such as: physiotherapists, rheumatologists, counsellors, Mental Health Teams and Pain Management.
- Make sure all letters say what treatment you are having or going to have.
- What is the outcome of these appointments?

When you go to the assessment, the assessor will not know you in any way. They will assess you on how you are at the meeting. Remember that the final decision is not given by them but what they write down influences it. A lot of the assessors have little to no medical training and are just following a list of questions.

Here are a few guidelines:

Look as you do on an average day.

Don't hide your pain; they need to see you how you feel.

If you are nervous, show it to the assessor.

If you fidget, then fidget.

If you need to cry, cry.

If you find eye contact difficult, avoid eye contact.

Don't hide anything that is normal to you. The assessor needs to see the real you.

As already mentioned, they will ask you many questions about your condition. It is easy to rush an answer and miss things out. Try not to.

As a general rule, tell them about how Fibby affects you on a bad day. They need to know what can happen, not only how you feel right now.

Take someone with you if you can, such as an advocate or partner. The charity provides this service to members. A friendly face and a small prompt can help if you get confused or upset. Stress will cause you to forget or clam up. It can also allow the FibroFog to happen.

Another good practice is to take a covering letter outlining the differences in you since the condition took over. This can be written by your family or partner and may help.

Ask if you need assistance. For example, if you find getting onto and off the toilet difficult, ask for help. This is also good to mention as balance problems come with Fibby.

Cooking may be an issue for you due to the period you have to stand, clumsiness or forgetfulness. Burning and scolding injuries are common for those with Fibby.

You may have trouble getting out of the house due to pain. Walking even short distances can be hard due to breathlessness.

Anxiety and depression can also cause problems with leaving the home.

Fibby can affect movement and co-ordination.

Maybe you have trouble getting out of bed or chairs. You may even spend days at a time in bed.

You may have sleep problems — not getting any or trouble staying awake.

Tell them everything. Remember that every word you say is written down, be honest and the credibility of the condition will shine through.

31. Learn to Say No

Do you find saying "no" is difficult? Do you feel guilty? You used to do those things all the time and cannot even contemplate them now.

Living with Fibby has far wider effects than people give credit for.

In this chapter, we are looking at the need to say no to people. These people could be family or friends, work colleagues or other outside influences.

We are not suggesting that it is easy. They may have known you before the condition and expect you to comply without a problem. Some examples might be:

No, I can't lend you money like I used to. I am on benefits now.

No, I can't have the grandchildren for the weekend as this would put me in bed for three days.

No, I can't socialise as I used to.

No, I really can't do it.

Why should we have to apologise for having Fibby? We never asked for Fibby to come and change our lives.

Be honest with yourself, your friends and family. Tell them how you feel thanks to Fibby and his lifestyle.

32. Try a Hobby or Activity

Hobbies and activities can help you cope with Fibby. You may be wondering, "What hobby could I do without aggravating my pain?"

Here are a few suggestions:

Crosswords

This is a good way of keeping the grey matter active.

Gentle exercise

Walk around your garden. Walk around your home, stopping at each window or room. Try to think of something nice, good or funny that has happened at each location. This will exercise you both the physically and emotionally and should build you up again.

Hobbies

You may want to try to knitting or crochet — skills often neglected due to the pace of life. It is lovely to see something made by your own hands. It may take a while to grow. And it may have odd holes in it for the first few tries!

As you can see, there are a few things that you could try — fun things and cheap things. Don't allow your body and mind to decay. It is easy to sit around feeling sorry for yourself but it won't help.

33. Try Keeping a Diary

Many people in our groups have found keeping a diary useful. This is an example of the type of information to include:

Date
Time
What hurts
Food
Anything done different

This sort of thing helps keep a record, not only for you but to give to your doctor. The more you write, the better the chance of seeing what might be triggering flare-ups and other symptoms, including extreme exhaustion.

Other diary details people use:

How was I feeling?

Stressed, fatigue, depressed, hot, cold, anxious.

Weather at time of change

Hot, cold, wet, dry, humid.

What food did I have?

Breakfast, lunch, dinner, supper, snack.

What position was my body in? Did the posture make a difference?

Sitting, standing, bending over, lying down, on my knees.

Severity of pain

0-1: Mild or no pain

2-3: Annoying pain

4-5: Uncomfortable pain

6-7: Distressing pain

8-9: Intense pain

10: Worst pain

How often did the pain occur? Did exercise bring on the symptoms?

Pain, migraine, fatigue, dizziness, breathlessness.

Sleeping

Was your sleep disturbed? Did you sleep at all? How many hours of sleep did you get? Did the mattress or pillows contribute to the cause?

Any diary works best over a four-week period. When you write everything down, it makes seeing the things that have triggered and changed easier. It also helps to see what does and does not help. Any changes that have occurred for the better can be put into daily living, so things will start to improve and become easier. Small things such as a food change can make a big difference.

This diary can also be helpful when seeing other professionals. Fibby is a complicated condition and showing the diary may allow them to get a better picture of how to help you. It may even show other problems to them.

As we always say:

"Anything that helps is better than nothing."

34. Looking for Support

As trustees of Cardiff and Vale Fibrofighters, we feel that finding a support group specific to your condition is very important.

A support group allows you a chance to mix with others. Even if you only want a tea or coffee, that is fine with us. You don't need to say anything, just listen.

We understand that the thought of walking into a new group is difficult for some sufferers. If this is you, arrange a phone call first by getting in touch on our Facebook or website. This way you won't feel alone. We can meet you individually somewhere first, if that helps. We can meet you outside the meeting and walk in with you, too. The important thing is to meet and share your experiences.

You will soon realise that you are not alone and that there are many more coping with this condition who want to help you.

Fibromyalgia is hard enough at the best of times. We try to make our support groups (as far as practical) non-Fibby. What we mean by this is that if Fibby needs to be mentioned, mention it. We will sort out the problem, then the subject is closed. Mostly, we talk about anything and everything in a light-hearted fashion, allowing for relaxation, companionship, fun and laughter.

Laughter is the best medicine!

35. Useful Contacts

www.fmauk.org

Fibromyalgia Action UK. Information website. Also has a list of support groups via their co-ordinators.

Cardiffandvalefibrofighters.org.uk

TheCardiffandValeFibrofighters@hotmail.com

All the information needed on where in South Wales our support groups are. We also do setup outside of area groups under our banner. These groups are run by each area.

www.fswales.org

FibroSupport-Wales is an online support forum offering advice and information to Fibby sufferers.

www.citizensadvice.org.uk

Citizens Advice Bureau, telephone 03444 111 444 or 0345 04 05 06.

www.gov.uk

The UK government website, for details of benefits.

Telephone ESA 0800 055 6688 and PIP 0800 917 2222

mind.org.uk

Mind is one of the UK's leading mental health charities. Telephone 0300 123 3393.

talktofrank.com

FRANK is a national advisory service for drug

problems. Telephone 0300 123 6600.

centrepoint.org.uk

Centrepoint helps homeless young people, aged sixteen to twenty-five. Telephone 0808 800 0661.

sheltercymru.org.uk

Shelter helps homeless people of all ages and advises on all types of housing issues. Telephone 08000 495 495.

samaritans.org

For emotional support any time, telephone 116 123 (free).

rethink.org

Rethink offers advice and support for mental illness issues. Telephone 0300 5000 927.

Community Advice and Listening Line

CALL is a mental health helpline for Wales, open 24/7/365, offering listening, information and support. Telephone 0800 132 737 or text "help" to 81066.

anxietyuk.org.uk

National charity helping people with anxiety. Telephone 0344 775 774.

theibsnetwork.org

National charity for IBS information, support and advice. Telephone 0114 272 3253.

bladderandbowel.org

The Bladder and Bowel Foundation offers support, information and guidance on bladder and bowel issues. Telephone 01536 533 255 or 0845 345 0165 for the helpline.

36. Research Resources

As we wrote this book, we trustees have learnt a lot about different things to do with Fibromyalgia. We used many reference points from recognised websites:

NHS Website

FMA UK

MedicalNewsToday.com

WebMD

Healthline.com

DWP website

Fibro.org.uk

There are many sites out there, but let me say this again:

Please speak to your doctor before trying new things.

We also recommend a book called The Englishman with Fibromyalgia by Shane Elliott Town. We found this book an easy read and it was the first book we read when diagnosed. It was also a little bit of encouragement to start the charity. Many members have enjoyed it, too.

We hope you found our book helpful.

37. Summing up Fibby

Frustration
Irritable
Bruised
Rubbish
Outcast
Moody
Yuck
Aches
Lonely
Grumpy
Insomnia
Awful

So please remember that even though you can't see it, we do Suffer.

38. Stories from Our Members

Fibromyalgia is a hidden illness that affects you inside and out. Nobody could imagine the pain you go through on a daily basis or how debilitating the illness is. People do not understand what you are going through and so treat you as if you are normal when, of course, you are not.

The inflammation affects your stomach and bowels as well as tendons, nerves, muscles and joints. It is a completely debilitating illness for which there is no cure. It affects your mental health and sufferers are often depressed as living with the illness can be so difficult, as there is no light at the end of the tunnel.

Linda H.

Four and a half years ago I got weakness in one leg, random falls from it, then pins and needles in my fingers and occasional numbness which resulted in dropping things like plates, getting smashed on regular occasions.

One night, I laid on the sofa and told my husband I had pain in my lower back and legs… It then turned into more than a pain, it felt like I was going to die! There are no words that can describe that sort of pain. I ended up in Cardiff hospital for nine hours with no answers and then was sent home, where I quickly recovered and was majorly relieved. That was it — or so I thought. One random lot of pain and it had gone. Nothing for the rest of the year.

However, something I had heard in the past from someone that had sudden weakness in one leg and with a member of the family having MS worried me. On a trip to Iran (I was living out there at this time), I went to have an MRI scan of my back and head and got the all clear. No growths or lesions on my brain or spine. This helped me relax a lot more about the possibility of MS.

However, year two was a little different as these "attacks" of pain started to happen every few months. As I went into hospital, they began thinking it was kidney stones… Apparently where the pain was starting from was where my kidneys are and the amount of pain I was in and the fact that I could stay still from it was common.

So, a CT scan cleared that up and I was sent home at two in the morning, saying they couldn't find a cause for my pain and I should take paracetamol.

Over time, things progressed awfully. The pain, the weakness and the chronic fatigue that affected me looking after my children. The forgetfulness is horrible too; imagine putting on an alarm on your phone, not to remind you to pick something up from the shops or for dinner, but an alarm to remember to pick your own children up from school! Before all this happened, I was an active mum of two, enjoying life, went everywhere with my kids and enjoyed a jog and the gym.

The gym times began to be too difficult as the recovery time from the workouts was just too long. I was exhausted and sore and could not walk properly for days afterwards, So I quit my membership and stopped jogging. So still the possibility of MS.

A much worse and a much more frightening idea, I know.

I must say that I am grateful that what I have isn't that. There is a family history of MS so I explained my concerns to the doctor again. She began to do her best to help me get to the bottom of it. The tests, however, were taking too long. Waiting lists of weeks and months were frustrating and I just could not cope with the pain any longer. So, my mum paid for me to see a private neurologist.

Test one: blood. Test two: x-ray. Test three: MRI. Test four (the worst): lumbar puncture.

Private neurologist, private rheumatologist.

Lumbar puncture… If anyone needs this, I am so sorry. I hated the experience, holding on to my mum's hand for dear life and begging them to stop until it was over.

Waiting for the results was hard but getting the all clear gave me mixed feelings.

Thank God that I don't have MS, but still no answers? What on earth could it be? After the private neurologist and all the tests that came with it, we were told to go and see the rheumatologist. One twenty-minute meeting later in which I was asked about stress in my past (I have had more than my share but it doesn't affect me now), a poke here and there on my body and touching my toes resulted in a diagnosis:

"Well, with your past and present stresses, I would say you have Fibromyalgia."

That was that, a referral to a pain management clinic

and a tiny booklet letting me know that this illness is incurable and can be treated with lots of pain killers, antidepressants and physiotherapy. That's it then, see you around. That is my story.

However, through the darkness came a light: my fantastic friends and wonderful support group, the Cardiff and Vale FibroFighters. With their help, I have been able to get out again and find new friends who relate to the pain, exhaustion and mental wellbeing, a group of people who are always there for each other whether Fibro-related or not. I know I can always call, text or email and someone will be there to help. They have been my rock through some of the hardest times and I will be forever grateful. I hope I have friends for life.

My Monday morning meet-ups with these guys are my highlight of the week — having a good laugh, a lovely cup of coffee and knowing you won't be judged is a great experience.

Ami P